GREEN PATRIOT POST- ERS

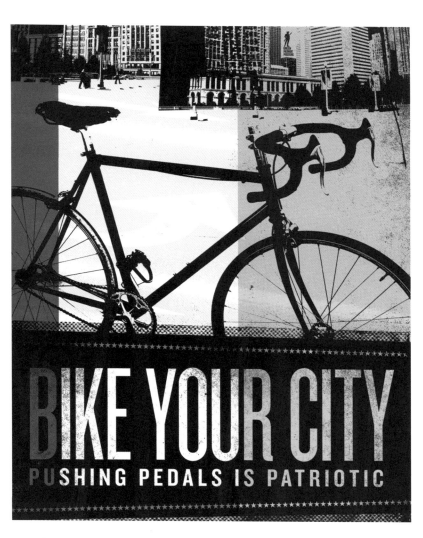

In association with **ENVIRONMENTAL DEFENSE FUND** and **THE CANARY PROJECT**

GREEN PATRIOT POSTERS

GRAPHICS FOR A SUSTAINABLE COMMUNITY

DMITRI SIEGEL & EDWARD MORRIS

With 68 colour illustrations

Thames & Hudson

CON-
TENTS

get
growing!
the
net a
greener
place!

ALL FUEL IS SCAR

ALBERT DORNE

ROW YOUR OW

A VICTORY GARDEN

PLAN FOR WINTER NO

NOV 8 1942

S ADMINISTRATION FOR WAR UR

YOUR HOME! Insulate walls an
storm doors, sas

R HEATING PLANT! Clean and r
Install fuel

EL AT ONCE! Take your dealer's advice
kind of fuel. Be ready to

**WAR SHIPMENTS
MEAN LESS
FUEL FOR ALL**

Dress warmly indoors

AVOID COLDS

**OUR FO
IS FIGHT**

L MAKE YOUR RATION

DESTROY THIS BOOK

MOST PEOPLE JUST DON'T get climate change. Few grasp the need and, more important, the opportunity to transform our society. So the people who do get it need to be louder, more insistent, and more effective at getting the message across.

This is predominantly a framing problem, and a framing problem is, in essence, a marketing problem. With the Green Patriot Posters project we looked to the graphic design and artistic communities for ways to invigorate and mobilize people to remake our economy for a more sustainable future. We wanted to contribute something to the rebranding of contemporary environmentalism, bringing climate change and the drive for clean energy to center stage and minimizing fearmongering about eco-apocalypse and mushy anthropomorphism of "Mother Earth" with their hand-me-down aesthetics and naive obsessions.

With this in mind we set out to collect and commission posters that created a stronger, more urgent, and more relevant movement. Like most people looking to build something from scratch, we started with our friends and branched out from there.

Where Is the Third Wave?
This year we celebrated the fortieth anniversary of Earth Day in the United States, but of course the environmental movement in this country is much older than that.

In a 1986 *Wall Street Journal* editorial, Fred Krupp of Environmental Defense Fund broke down the history of the movement into three "waves." The first wave, he wrote, "was a reaction to truly rapacious exploitation of natural resources in the wake of the Industrial Revolution" and the focus then "was on conservation, stemming the loss of forest lands and wildlife, especially in the West." The second wave "recognized that the contamination of water, land, and air had sown seeds of destruction for both wildlife and humans. The strategy in this second phase has been to try to halt abusive pollution."

The first two waves had great success. First wave: the creation of our National Forests, the passage of the Wilderness Act of 1964; second wave: the passage of the Clean Air Act, the creation of the Environmental Protection Agency. Our air and water are cleaner and more land is protected. Our very consciousness about the environment has changed. We have become more sensitive to ecology.

Yet Krupp was right to point out that the environmental movement needed a new direction, a third wave, and that the old paradigms starkly opposing industry and nature were worn out and counterproductive. An emphasis on conservation and purity made the movement seem precious and out of touch. Not far off were the cries concerning "the end of nature" and "the death of environmentalism" (both titles of books that would be published in the years to come).

The problem is that twenty years later the focus has been found, but the strategy has not. Climate change is clearly the challenge of our times, but is the environmental movement doing a good job of motivating the public to address it? In our view, despite its successful history and the urgency of its current agenda, the environmental movement has not evolved to meet the challenge of this third wave. It is broad but weak—weaker than it should be given the imperative of its message.

It is a movement that primarily seems to concern affluent people in mostly superficial ways. Younger people, who are the real stakeholders given that they will inherit an environment on the verge of collapse, are weirdly apathetic, hedonistic, and cynical. Less affluent people, who are the most likely to feel the impacts of climate change—crashing economies and starvation—can't find enough head-space for these concerns in a world overcrowded with anxieties. Conservatives have become convinced that this once nonpartisan issue is now a threat to their core values. America's future is at stake and precious few seem to really care or even understand.

Why Graphic Design?
So why graphic design? What can it do? The inspiration came first from WPA (Works Progress Administration) and World War II posters. During the war the United States was able to mobilize industry and its citizens with breathtaking speed. Factories were overhauled and consumption habits were transformed. Conservation (in the form of rationing) became a patriotic act. Strong, graphically compelling post-

ers played a crucial role in the success of this campaign. In these posters, taking action was presented as vital for the good of the nation, and those who were willing to sacrifice were portrayed as dynamic American heroes. This is just what we need today.

Contrast the power and effectiveness of these World War II images with some of the current visual media in the environmental advocacy realm. In the latter there are essentially three modes: 1) Save the Earth (which to us seems meaningless and apparently strikes the general public as crying wolf); 2) Save the animals (not meaningless at all, but dodges the crux of the matter: future human suffering vs. continued human prosperity); 3) Eco-apocalypse (a legitimate possibility, but a trope that often feels whiny and too distant to be actionable). All of these strategies also suffer from the fact that by the time their truth is tangible to the public it will be far, far too late.

So what is right for our time? We took the approach that no one person knows the answer, and that is why we opened up the project to multiple designers and to the general public. But the posters we selected for this book represent a particular vision—the vision of the editors. We believe that graphic design does not just respond to the zeitgeist— it helps shape it. With that in mind we generally sought posters that convey urgency and/or optimism (in a word: strength), but we remained open about the specific content or imagery we received.

Working with Irony, Cynicism, and Attention Deficit
Conceptual problems and lingering clichés were not the only obstacles we faced as we began to wade into the design community. Society has changed since the environmental movements of the '60s and '70s and, of course, it has changed even more since World War II. Our culture has become extremely skeptical of, even hostile to, sincerity, conviction, and inspiration. Visual culture is dominated by irony, detachment, and snark. Idealism in visual communication is perceived as phony and quickly parsed for inconsistency and hypocrisy. Designers and marketers have created a visual culture that is almost toxic for advocacy.

Brazen dishonesty in advertising and branding have made the public rightly suspicious, but perhaps more pernicious is the fact that once that dishonesty became widely understood, it was replaced with a kind of self-referential nothingness. Ads are filled with nonsequiturs, boring office set-ups, and talking babies. Graphic design has become glib and self-deprecating in the extreme. Dishonesty has been replaced with a void.

Part of the reason for this void is the lack of institutions with the cultural or social authority to back up a call to action. The World War II posters we were inspired by were effective partly because there was confidence in our government and the industries that supported the war effort. People were likely not only to trust the government, but also to feel a sense of common purpose with it. Today virtually all institutions—government, the military, the press, big business—are viewed with suspicion, if not hostility. Environmental activists deserve some of the blame for this. Legitimate criticism and protest have evolved into a culture of knee-jerk antibusiness, antigovernment conspiracy theories to the point where all big institutions (even large environmental organizations) are considered illegitimate because of their size. Unfortunately we will need big institutions and mass organization to get us out of this mess.

Such deep-seated cynicism created one of the core challenges that faced this project. It was clear that no institutional partner or media sponsor would likely inspire meaningful participation. In our networked culture it is the individual that has credibility, not institutions. People trust their friends; they don't trust the government. Consensus comes in the form of a mesh of likes, links, comments, and recommendations. The institutional has been replaced with the social. To be credible we had to make our own mini–social network that enabled the authority and credibility of the community to guide the project. The Green Patriot Posters website enables peer-to-peer creation and valuation of images through online submissions, community-based voting, and frictionless sharing across social networks.

Miniature Monuments

Basing a poster project around a website seemed like a bit of a contradiction. The obvious question (one that came at us often) was, "Why posters"? The web has not only changed how consensus and community work; it has become the dominant medium for visual communication as well. Posters were traditionally a way of dominating public spaces like street corners and bus stations, but now our public space is online. How does a poster work in a world where it is more likely to be seen on a Facebook wall than an actual wall?

One fundamental principle of this project is that the poster has retained the power and impact of its roots even as it has been squashed down into a jpg. The idea of the poster has survived even as the context and medium have shifted. This is partly because, ironically, the design challenge of making something impactful in a Twitter feed is very similar to that of making something readable from across the street. It requires scale, contrast, and bold messaging. In the endless stream of information and updates that characterizes the web, the visual properties of a poster are quite effective—they are miniature monuments. Each online poster also serves as a thumbnail for a bigger idea,

a hyperlink to the greater project of fighting climate change. Building a better button is now more important than building a better mousetrap. A clever or arresting poster design garners clicks; the quality of its design is a call to action in and of itself—"click here."

The Obama Campaign and Fairey's *Hope* Poster

The relative weakness of the environmental movement, the lack of credible public institutions, and the fracturing of our culture into a peer-to-peer network made us doubtful that public art or cause-related imagery could have a meaningful impact in fighting climate change. But Barack Obama's campaign for president changed that. For the first time in a generation, there was a cause, a movement, an institution that young people felt was worthy of not just trust, but also action and personal sacrifice.

And a poster played a major role in that campaign. Shepard Fairey's poster *Hope* demonstrated that an unironic, idealistic image could take hold in our culture and inspire people, particularly young people, the way World War II posters had. It was the widespread embrace of that image and the vision of young people volunteering on the campaign and voting in record numbers that made us feel like a poster might actually be able to contribute to a broader movement for sustainability and the fight against climate change.

Our hope has been affirmed by the quality and the sheer number of poster designs that continue to flow into the Green Patriot Posters website. Clearly there is a great deal of interest in rallying around the fight against climate change to create a more sustainable future.

What We Got

As posters started rolling in some inspired us, some depressed us, and some just confused us. But several topics recurred, including bicycles, local food, and renewable energy/the end of oil. Notably each of these is positive, solution-oriented, visualizable, and realizable, and each gives distinct agency to the individual.

The bicycle is a nonthreatening, nonideological image, unsanctimonious and almost childlike. At the same time its mere presence is a direct challenge to our car culture, which drives so much CO_2 into our atmosphere. It is also a symbol of individual responsibility and empowerment in the face of an overwhelming challenge. As we mentioned above, the individual is the most meaningful institution in our culture today, so it is probably no coincidence that the bicycle—a vehicle built for one—would be so resonant.

Posters about local food were among the most fun and the most inclined to employ retro imagery—a reminder that the values of this movement have deep roots in American society.

Alternative technologies were valorized in many of the posters, including Fairey's iconic windmill. These images reflect a faith that technology and innovation are the great assets of America that will surmount the challenge of climate change—an interesting update to the qualities of determination, grit, and resourcefulness, which were the focus of the World War II–era posters. These works represent a yearning for a different kind of industry, one that harnesses technology, capital, and innovation in the interest of more than just shareholder value—actual *values*. There is clearly an opportunity for energy companies to replace reckless, shameless practices like deep-water drilling with clean-energy exploration.

Not surprisingly, many designers, particularly many of the youngest designers, deftly adapted the humor and irony that dominate our culture to the cause, hijacking this vernacular for a higher purpose. Jeremy Dean's co-opted rap lyric in *It's Getting Hot in Here* and Xander Pollock's melting of Al Gore's face proved that a contemporary environmental movement needs to speak in a contemporary language. Several designers, perhaps frustrated with the lack of credible institutions, made up fictitious ones—Eric Benson's Renewable Electrification Administration, DJ Spooky's People's Republic of Antarctica.

Yet what struck us the most was the polyphonic nature of the submissions. There is no one prevailing ethos, aesthetic, or message. We see this as a strength, not a weakness. It is a sign of the times and of what is needed to invigorate the environmental movement to address the challenges of climate change and energy independence: flexibility, dynamism, and the embrace of complexity and multiplicity.

Making the Book
As the posters piled up, the pressure mounted to compile the best of the best into a book. We were skeptical. We have a lot of books. They generally sit on the shelf or in a pile. For a project that was dedicated to action and reducing consumption, how could we justify producing something that would consume a lot of energy and resources largely to fill shelf space?

We decided that if we were going to make a book, it had to have a purpose consistent with the project overall, and it had to be printed sustainably. Working with Monroe Litho in Rochester, New York, we set the page count and trim size to minimize waste in the printing process. The book was printed domestically, using 100 percent wind-generated electricity (through the purchase of Green-e certified renewable energy certificates); vegetable-based inks; and paper that is made in New York with 100 percent post-consumer recycled material, 100 percent wind-generated electricity, and is FSC (Forestry Stewardship Council) certified.

(The cover paper is made with 80 percent post-consumer recycled material.)

Yet financial realities being what they are, the publisher could not afford to print a book this way and stay in business. So we had to search for funders. In other words we created an artificial economy through donor intervention. Those donors, who deserve as much credit for this book as anyone, are: Environmental Defense Fund, Richard H. Goodwin, Judith Bell, Neva Goodwin, Gabe Nugent, Hiscock & Barclay, and an anonymous source. It bears emphasizing that a subsidy from donors is not a good long-term solution to any business problem. Ultimately more publishers, more businesses, have to be committed to doing things the right way (making fewer books at a higher price, or whatever it takes) to move the economy in the right direction. It would not be so expensive to print sustainably if there was higher demand for it.

In making the book we felt that in order for it to be meaningful, it had to be active. For this reason we wanted the posters to be detachable and spreadable. In this way the book becomes a means of distribution and personalization, and a source of energy. We want you to destroy this book. We hope you will tear out the pages and display them, in your room, your office, your locker—wherever. We did not want to make a monument or a historical record; the website will serve as a more effective and public monument to the project. We wanted to distribute the posters and give people an affordable way to own and display them.

What Do I Do Now?
Obviously the poster itself does not create the change we need. That takes people. So what do we hope is the outcome of our book? Real movement-building. And that takes time. If you are inspired by a poster, tear it out and hang it up. Or carry it at a protest. Or find it on our website and pass it on digitally. Make your own poster. Post it. Let it enter the culture and begin its work changing consciousness.

If you want to do more, do it. On the back of each poster is a link to "Go Further" with an idea or action represented in the design. Creating a strong, visible sentiment that raises eyebrows and pushes markets and policy is work in and of itself. But this book is not just about graphic design; it's about making real change. Follow a few of the links in the book. Act—and urge others to do the same.

Hold yourself and others accountable. The most important people to hold accountable are your elected officials. Contact your representatives; organize a demonstration or other local action. Be louder, more insistent, and more persistent. Create the third wave. The ball is in your court. •

THOMAS L. FRIEDMAN

THE P-OWER OF GREEN

IN THE WORLD OF IDEAS, to name something is to own it. If you can name an issue, you can own the issue. One thing that always struck me about the term "green" was the degree to which, for so many years, it was defined by its opponents—by the people who wanted to disparage it. And they defined it as "liberal," "tree-hugging," "sissy," "girlie-man," "unpatriotic," "vaguely French."

Well, I want to rename "green." I want to rename it geostrategic, geoeconomic, capitalistic, and patriotic. I want to do that because I think that living, working, designing, manufacturing, and projecting America in a green way can be the basis of a new unifying political movement for the twenty-first century. A redefined, broader, and more muscular green ideology is not meant to trump the traditional Republican and Democratic agendas but rather to bridge them

when it comes to addressing the three major issues facing every American today: jobs, temperature, and terrorism.

How do our kids compete in a flatter world? How do they thrive in a warmer world? How do they survive in a more dangerous world? Those are, in a nutshell, the big questions facing America at the dawn of the twenty-first century. But these problems are so large in scale that they can only be effectively addressed by an America with fifty green states—not an America divided between red and blue states.

Because a new green ideology, properly defined, has the power to mobilize liberals and conservatives, evangelicals and atheists, big business and environmentalists around an agenda that can both pull us together and propel us forward. That's why I say: We don't just need the first black president. We need the first green president. We don't just need the first woman president. We need the first environmental president. We don't just need a president who has been toughened by years as a prisoner of war but a president who is tough enough to level with the American people about the profound economic, geopolitical, and climate threats posed by our addiction to oil—and to offer a real plan to reduce our dependence on fossil fuels.

After World War II, President Eisenhower responded to the threat of Communism and the "red menace" with massive spending on an interstate highway system to tie America together, in large part so that we could better move weapons in the event of a war with the Soviets. That highway system, though, helped enshrine America's car culture (atrophying our railroads) and lock in suburban sprawl and low-density housing, which all combined to get America addicted to cheap fossil fuels, particularly oil. Many in the world followed our model.

Today we are paying the accumulated economic, geopolitical, and climate prices for that kind of America. I am not proposing that we radically alter our lifestyles. We are who we are—including a car culture. But if we want to continue to be who we are, enjoy the benefits, and be able to pass them on to our children, we do need to fuel our future in a cleaner, greener way. Eisenhower rallied us with the red menace. Obama will have to rally us with a green patriotism. Hence my motto: "Green is the new red, white, and blue."

Green is not about cutting back. It's about creating a new cornucopia of abundance for the next generation by inventing a whole new industry. It's about getting our best brains out of hedge funds and into innovations that will give us not only the clean-power industrial assets to preserve our American dream but also the technologies that billions of others need to realize their own dreams without destroying the planet. It's about making America safer by breaking our addiction to a fuel that is powering regimes deeply hostile to our values. And, finally, it's about making America the global environmental leader, instead of laggard, which as Arnold Schwarzenegger argues would "create a very powerful side product." Those who dislike America because of Iraq, he explained, would at least be able to say, "Well, I don't like them for the war, but I do like them because they show such unbelievable leadership—not just with their blue jeans and hamburgers but with the environment. People will love us for that. That's not existing right now."

As John Hennessy, the president of Stanford, taught me: Confronting this climate-energy issue is the epitome of what John Gardner, the founder of Common Cause, once described as "a series of great opportunities disguised as insoluble problems." Am I optimistic? I want to be. But I am also old-fashioned. I don't believe the world will effectively address the climate-energy challenge without America, its president, its government, its industry, its markets, and its people all leading the parade. Green has to become part of America's DNA. We're getting there. Green has hit Main Street—it's now more than a hobby—but it's still less than a new way of life.

Why? Because big transformations—women's suffrage, for instance—usually happen when a lot of aggrieved people take to the streets, the politicians react, and laws get changed. But the climate-energy debate is more muted and slow moving. Why? Because the people who will be most harmed by the climate-energy crisis haven't been born yet. "This issue doesn't pit haves versus have-nots," notes the Johns Hopkins foreign policy expert Michael Mandelbaum, "but the present versus the future—today's generation versus its kids and unborn grandchildren." Once the Geo-Green interest group comes of age, especially if it is after another 9/11 or Katrina, Mandelbaum said, "it will be the biggest interest group in history—but by then it could be too late."

An unusual situation like this calls for the ethic of stewardship. Stewardship is what parents do for their kids: think about the long term, so they can have a better future. It is much easier to get families to do that than whole societies, but that is our challenge. In many ways our parents rose to such a challenge in World War II—when an entire generation mobilized to preserve our way of life. That is why they were called the Greatest Generation. Our kids will only call us the Greatest Generation if we rise to our challenge and become the Greenest Generation. •

Excerpted from Thomas L. Friedman, "The Power of Green," *New York Times Magazine*, April 15, 2007.

STEVEN HELLER

WHY POST-ERS?

ISN'T PRINT DEAD YET?

IMAGINE TWENTIETH-CENTURY

America before television. It was a Dark Age indeed. People had to make do with reading and conjuring mental pictures. There were, of course, radio and films, but the instantaneous transmission of picture *and* sound was impossible (although the Nazis experimented with TV and even video telephones as early as 1936). No continually broadcasting LEDs existed. Nor were there electronically generated data streams (despite the employ of ticker-tape machines). Nonetheless, even in the absence of flat-screen TVs, there were flat walls on which to post words and images. This was a time when posters had a huge impact on the mass consciousness.

In fact the vast majority of national and patriotic propaganda—both cautionary and informational—was received through posters produced by government agencies, like the Office of War Information during the early 1940s. The missives ranged from how to avoid colds to how to avoid sabotage, from how to grow food to how to grow armament. Posters were at times artful and artless. They shouted out to the worker and student, civilian and soldier, and all other passersby. They imparted what was important in order for Americans to be responsible citizens. Needless to say, posters were everywhere because TV and computers were not.

But today the poster is a vestige of what it once was. Paper? Isn't that supposed to be a dying resource? Print? Isn't it dead yet?

Today there are many platforms for sending and receiving information. Too many! In fact, frequently, we are more likely to miss important messages as they fly by our eyes in clever animated Flash sequences or rotating decks on the web. Bells and whistles trump form. Form often trumps content. These days the medium is indeed the message.

Which is why the venerable poster retains its resonance and relevancy. Posters literally stick around (at least until they are torn down or defaced) for some time. Many of the posters produced during World War I, the Great Depression, and World War II are still with us in pictures in books and on postcards, in museums and libraries—and on "remixes" of vintage imagery with contemporary messages. The more familiar images become accepted icons. The more startling slogans become vernacular ("I Want You!" or "Loose Lips Sink Ships"). Posters are ingrained in our minds and histories. Certainly the posters in this very collection are, in part, drawn from the history of posters; some borrow techniques and images of the past while others build upon the legacy with new and innovative concepts.

A poster enables the maker to load as much or as little visual and textual information as needed. More important, in this media-saturated environment, it allows the viewer to spend as much or as little time with it as necessary. Contemplation breeds intelligent action, not simply a rote reaction. Which is not to say that TV, cable, and the Internet—websites, blogs, and tweets—are ineffective. These reach many more people than virtually any poster ever produced. And yet we don't hang websites, blogs, and tweets on the wall or refrigerator. A poster continues to have totemic status. If done well (and that must be a prerequisite), the poster will continue to be effective, efficient, and emblematic of the cause or issue it represents. What's more, posters now live in apparent perpetuity on the web as well.

Is producing Green Patriot posters an effective way of making a positive mark on the planet—or another blemish? Is it counterintuitive to the goals of environmental activism—or a viable means to trigger action? What's different about posters today from yesterday is the fundamental question of waste. In the Dark Age no one gave a whit about such matters. During our current Enlightenment it is foremost on people's minds. Still, despite their ephemeral nature, posters are an essential medium. Despite what the naysayers may say, posters enter a realm of consciousness that is much harder for the fleeting digital image to reach. •

MORGAN CLENDANIEL

GREEN MEANS GO

ON EARTH DAY IN 1971, Keep America Beautiful ran an advertisement that, in many ways, changed the face of the environmental movement in America. It's become one of those pieces of popular culture that is burned so indelibly into our collective consciousness that even people who were not alive when it aired have memories of it. You know it well: A weathered Native American travels by canoe from the bucolic countryside to a trash-infested urban landscape, whereupon he turns to the camera and sheds a single tear.

According to the Ad Council, the "Crying Indian" ad helped inspire volunteers to reduce litter by as much as 88 per-

cent in thirty-eight states. Whether or not those miraculous results are possible, the ad's larger importance is unmistakable: It showed that, when presented emotionally rather than factually, green issues could make a far more effective impression than the environmental movement had been able to do until then.

But would an ad like that work today, when the environmental issues we face are far more dire than pervasive litter? Could someone make a piece of media about the fact that while climate change threatens our very existence as a species, many people and governments on Earth seem unwilling to admit the problem exists, let alone confront it with the level of seriousness and purpose it requires? And could this piece be so powerful that it drastically changes people's behavior?

The young people of today—a mix of the youngest of Generation Y and the oldest of the Millennials—are the ones who have to galvanize into a cohesive movement to fight climate change and convince our governments to do so. Our parents' generation did it during the 1960s and 1970s. What would it take to mobilize young people today?

We are always portrayed as an incredibly media-savvy and well-informed generation. But our point-and-click culture has also left us with an expectation of real-time results. The protests of our parents' generation slowly led, one by one, to tangible changes. We are more jaded and demanding. So when we see a protest that doesn't result in an instant change in policy, it seems, perhaps, a little pointless. After the last ten years of protests about everything from the war in Iraq to globalization to COP15, the whole idea begins to seem fruitless. We know climate change is bad, but going out and yelling about it doesn't get the kind of measurable instant results we've come to expect.

And it's not a question of education. Anyone who cares to know can download the relevant climate-change facts. But the glut of information at our fingertips is too much to put one issue in stark enough relief to make it stand out. We are a generation that cares deeply about issues and doing good, but sometimes we care more about "the issues" to the detriment of caring about any one issue in particular. Climate change is just one item in a litany of horrible problems we know something needs to be done about. That it could destroy life on this planet, and thus should take precedent over other concerns, is sometimes hard to wrap your head around, especially when confronted with whatever celebrity has recently attached himself or herself to another cause. There is no sense of urgency. Our parents knew people who went to Vietnam and didn't come back. Our summers seem like they might be getting a little warmer. Yet there is nothing to push us past our general sense of mild concern and to get us on the phones with our representatives and into the streets en masse.

To involve young people in fighting climate change is going to take a new tactic.

What we do respond to, perhaps sadly, are branding and advertising. Our generation has sold out, happily, and we're reaping the benefits. We are inundated with corporate messages every day and instead of being disgusted we take advantage. Unlike earlier generations of young people, with us any distrust of massive conglomerates has dissipated, and we reward the companies that do the best job of appealing to us through their advertisements and actions.

But corporate America doesn't get to own those tactics. Just because corporations use a combination of good graphic design and a basic understanding of human psychology to sell more product doesn't mean it's inherently bad to use those tactics for anything else. The best graphic design connects on a visceral level that goes beyond being just eye candy; the best advertising concepts convince people of a need they didn't know they had. We can say that those methods should only be used to convince people that they must go out and buy more widgets, but why not also employ them to convince people they need to buy into collective action against climate change? It worked so well for litter in '71; there is no reason it can't work for climate change now. Give solving climate change the best branding, the best design, the best presentation, and a whole generation might better understand. Important, world-changing ideas can be presented just as accessibly and made just as interesting as any pop culture story. If you can make it look appealing, it becomes appealing, and more appealing means better understood.

Since the facts have so far failed to convince people, clearly another tactic is needed. Now that the scientists have sounded the warning—a warning that has thus far largely fallen on deaf ears—it's time to turn it over to the designers and other communicators. Let's go beyond just a rational appeal to people's brains; we must appeal to people's hearts.

It's a mindset that needs to continue to be embraced by the environmental movement. There is no reason to give up on the idea of mass appeal. We can present the issues viscerally without doing them a disservice. The posters in this book—images that appeal to us on a level deeper than any numbers or academic explanations can—represent the path down which the environmental movement needs to continue. Hopefully, like the crying Native American, people who are confronted with these human appeals about the dangers of climate change and the prospect of a better future will become more willing to admit the problem and embrace solutions. If you're reading this book, there is a good chance you are already willing to do something about climate change. But there are many who aren't. First we must convince people they need to care about the issue. We can talk about the science later. •

MICHAEL BIERUT

FIVE WAYS TO DE- SIGN FOR A CAUSE

GRAPHIC DESIGN, the field to which I've devoted my life, isn't mentioned often in popular fiction. A rare exception can be found in Richard Price's epic 600-page 1992 novel *Clockers*. In it Price tells the story of a young drug dealer, Strike, describing his desperate, day-to-day existence in harrowing detail. My profession makes its appearance while Strike is visiting his parole officer:

The walls of the waiting room were hung with black-and-white cautionary posters, encircling Strike with admonitions, the subjects ranging from AIDS to pregnancy to crack to alcohol, each one a little masterpiece of dread. Strike hated posters. If you were poor, posters followed you everywhere—health clinics, probation offices, housing offices, day care centers, welfare offices—and they were always blasting away at you with warnings to do this, don't do that, be like this, don't be like that, smarten up, control this, stop that.

That three-word sentence stopped me cold: "Strike hated posters." Graphic designers, as everybody knows, love posters. The difference between these two points of view couldn't be more disturbing to me. I love posters. I love looking at them, and I love designing them. By the time I'd read those words, I'd spent countless hours designing many of those "little masterpieces of dread." Bold. Black and white. Designed to, yes, blast away with their admonishing messages. I had to do some soul searching. Who was I designing for, anyway?

The poster for the pro bono cause is, frankly, a bit of a cliché in contemporary design practice. Like many others, I was always happy to take them on because of their meaty subject matter. Forget the struggle to find drama in inherently dull commercial subjects. Here, instead, were the great themes: life, death, good, evil, the very future of humanity. And my imaginary audience was, often, humanity itself. At least that's what I told myself. If I were completely honest, I'd admit that my real audience was one I know a little bit better: my fellow designers. Or perhaps even a more cynically limited subset: fellow designers who judge design competitions.

Right around the time I first read Price's words, I was ready to make some changes. Design for designers is great, but the real challenge in doing cause-related work is communicating with the larger public beyond our small circles. It's harder in every way: harder to compete with all the other noise, harder to reach the people who can really make a difference. This means thinking differently, in five specific ways.

One: Be clear about your purpose
If you're acting as a communicator, be clear about what you're communicating. "Building awareness" can be a cop-out, an excuse to separate cause and effect. What do you want your work to accomplish? How will you know if you're successful? Make your goal action, and determine the most direct way to provoke it. Be outrageously ruthless.

Two: Know your audience
Who are you trying to reach? Don't start until you have an answer to this question. A message that doesn't ring true—visually, verbally, and in every other way—will get dismissed or, even worse, ignored. Understand the context of the people who will be seeing your work. The more you can master that language, the more your message will get through.

Three: Try not to use design as therapy
When horrible things happen, feeling bad is an understandable reaction. Helping makes us feel better. Figure out the best way to help. Is making a poster the best way? Sometimes, donating your talent is great. Often, simply donating money is better.

Four: Don't be "creative"
The brilliant Chilean architect Alejandro Aravena says, "Creativity is what you do when there is not enough knowledge. If you have knowledge, you do not need creativity." Don't use work for social causes as a showcase for your cleverness, or as an excuse to stretch your creative muscles without the constraints of demanding clients. Do your research, get the knowledge you need, and then find the fastest, most bullshit-free route from point A to point B. If you can be clever on the way, go ahead—but not at the expense of getting your point across. Be your own demanding client.

Five: No matter what, be optimistic and positive
The best designs and the most effective campaigns are inspiring, not depressing. Don't admonish; don't talk down to people. At its best our work can serve as a rallying cry and give voice to people who might otherwise feel isolated and silent. Use your work to visualize the future, and lead the way with enthusiasm and passion.

There are lots of ways to design for a cause. No doubt each of the designers represented in this book has grappled with issues similar to mine. The Green Patriot Poster project shows how each has responded to the challenge on his or her own terms. Together these posters demonstrate that design can be a potent tool for communication and social transformation. And if you look hard enough, and think even harder, you, too, will find your own way. •

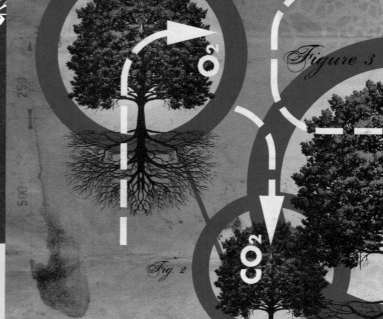

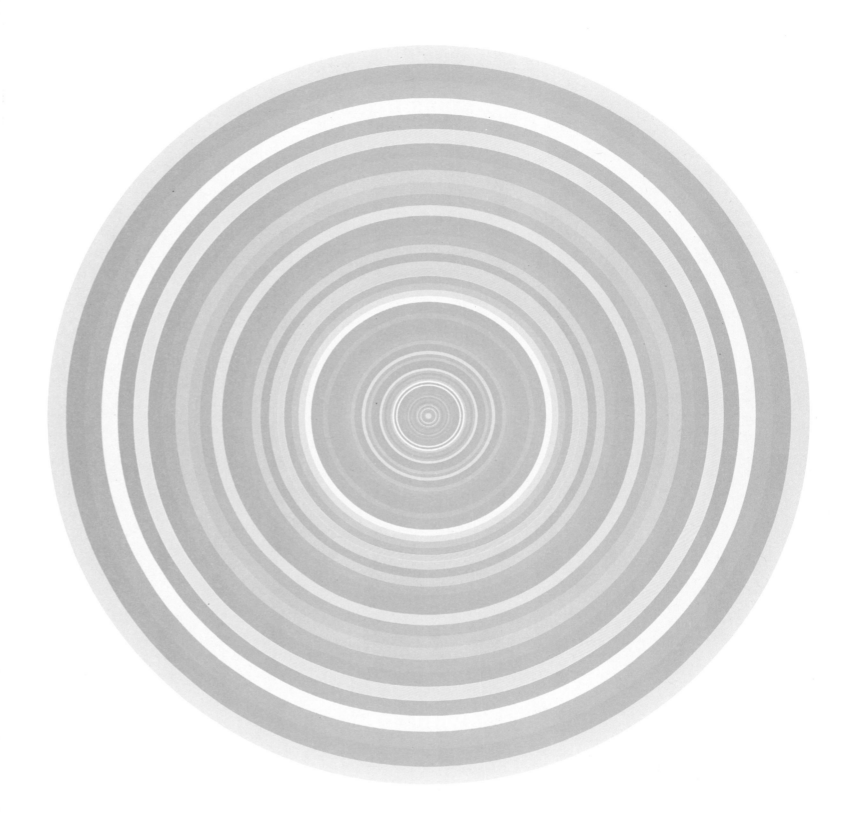

In the future,
green will be just another color.

THUMB | In the Future Green Will Be Just Another Color

"Green is a color, the perception of which is evoked by light in the visible spectrum at approximately 520 to 570 nanometers. At various times green has been culturally associated with life, fertility, rebirth, and those who are inexperienced or jealous. It may refer to money, traffic lights, political parties on either the left or right, and, lately, environmental awareness. In the future it will signify other things." –Thumb

GO FURTHER: www.nextnature.net

sprumer
sumumn
auter
winting

golab waminrg

MATHILDE FALLOT | Golab waminrg

"What if the seasons didn't mean anything anymore? And climate behaved unpredictably? You don't really want to hear about global warming but increasingly you will have to." –MF

Designed for the International Poster and Graphic Design Festival of Chaumont, 2007, in a workshop with Paul Sahre.

GO FURTHER: www.ipcc.ch

MIKE PERRY | Let Them Grow

"I really responded to the original WPA phrase 'Let it grow'—it seemed much bigger. I wanted to make something that lifted the spirits. It seems like the program should never have stopped." –MP

Design first appeared in *Readymade* magazine, 2009.

GO FURTHER: www.gearthblog.com/blog/archives/2008/06/disappearing_forests_google_earth_v.html

ESTEBAN CHAVEZ | Sustain

"It is a long and uncertain road, but there is light at the end of tunnel. It is up to all of us to make that light brighter." –EC

GO FURTHER: www.edf.org

GM2006

GEOFF McFETRIDGE | Lumberjack

"McFetridge's lumberjack drawing captures the quandary we all face in meeting the threat of cli-
mate change and creating a sustainable economy. The sprout on the lumberjack's toe challenges
his instincts and confronts him with a choice, just as we are confronted by a choice about how to
moderate our way of life in an interconnected world." –DS and EM

Designed for Patagonia, 2008.

GO FURTHER: www.patagonia.com/web/us/patagonia.go?slc=en_US&sct=US&assetid=1960

JON SANTOS | Washington Monument

"*Everyone admires the spirit and optimism of Buckminster Fuller. But what happens when the utopian dreams of the past don't come true—or even close to true? Do you lose faith? Become a cynic? Or do you conjure up new dreams and move on? What would happen if we no longer had images of a better future? How gray would the world become? After all, there is nothing extraordinarily far-fetched about windmills dotting our nation's capital. Yet what are we to make of flamingoes in the Washington Monument?*" –DS and EM

GO FURTHER: www.repoweramerica.org

DON'T BE STUCK UP!

Save energy, SWITCH OFF.

BRANDON SCHAEFER | Don't Be Stuck Up

"At one point or another, we've all turned up our noses at the idea of switching off our lights or other electrical devices when leaving a room. Like so many other things in the modern world, leaving on lights, computers, and other appliances has become a bad habit that many of us have had a hard time recognizing as such. The fact remains, though, that simply switching off unused lights can reduce energy consumed for lighting up to 45 percent, while also reducing several other kinds of environmental impact caused by electricity generation." –BS

GO FURTHER: www1.eere.energy.gov/consumer/tips

DIEGO GUTIÉRREZ | Keep Buying Shit

"To a graphic designer, there is no better reason to design than for a good cause. At the same time, popular media and kitsch design have exhausted a cause like global warming. Since Al Gore's movie An Inconvenient Truth *came out, it has become popular for commercial design to take green to the masses. Although for a good cause, these sorts of commercial iterations are still very often designed with fluff for fluffy brains—there is no true statement of the urgency with which we must act to keep our lifestyle or even the world as we know it. When I entered the Green Patriot Poster class at RISD, I wanted to take the opportunity to generate designs that would make an impact on whoever laid eyes on them. In other words I didn't want to design for upper-middle-class mothers who hang out at Whole Foods. My vision was to crank out as many varieties of strong images, harsh statements, and loud colors as I could." –DG*

Designed for Green Patriot Posters studio in bachelor of graphic design program at Rhode Island School of Design, 2009, taught by Nancy Skolos and critiqued by Edward Morris.

GO FURTHER: www.storyofstuff.com

KRISTINA KOSTADINOVA | Friend in Trouble

"I believe that to be a good designer these days, we should care! All senses wide open....Be aware, be awake, be in touch with the world all the time. Sense the weaknesses, feel the need, and send your message—a word, bold enough to be heard. Good graphic design must talk. This poster is an alarm. The Earth needs attention.

"Be a green patriot and don't stop at provocation—find the solutions. It is time to push ourselves out of the comfort zone and to say something louder." –KK

GO FURTHER: www.350.org

SHEPARD FAIREY | Power Up Windmill

"I believe very strongly that green energy is the only way for the United States to achieve energy independence, create valuable technology, and protect the environment. I created this windmill image as a patriotic symbol of the green energy mission. I am proud to team up with MoveOn to promote clean energy." –SF

Designed for moveon.org, 2009.

GO FURTHER: pol.moveon.org/call/oneoffs/index_1378.html?cp_id=1378

EVERYTHING STUDIO | Earth

"There are no passengers on Spaceship Earth. We are all crew." –Marshall McLuhan, 1964

GO FURTHER: www.bfi.org

FRÉDÉRIC TACER | Global Warming

"I wanted the poster to remind people, in a simple and efficient way, that by destroying the planet we're only destroying ourselves. And it is just a matter of time until we reap what we sow. I like to compare this picture to the story of the snake biting its own tail. That red fella is an obvious symbol of humanity. It is too late to look for the people to blame. We're all in this together." –FT

GO FURTHER: creationcare.org

MANIFESTO

אנטארקטיקה

FOR A PEOPLE'S REPUBLIC OF
ANTARCTICA

DJ SPOOKY (aka PAUL D. MILLER) | Manifesto for a People's Republic of Antarctica (part of Terra Nova: Sinfonia Antarctica)

"Antarctica has many faces: It's usually thought of as a huge pile of ice that somehow stays afloat at the bottom of the world. In different ages, before humanity had mapped out the world, it would have simply been beyond most maps and most ideas about what made up the geography of the world. Today Antarctica persists as a symbol of the unknown, and as such possesses great symbolic strength." –DJS

GO FURTHER: www.ipy.org

JASON HARDY | Let's Ride

"A bicycle is a beautifully simple machine. Two wheels, a frame, and a crank—that's all you need. So I wanted to make a simple poster celebrating one of those key components—the wheel. The call to action is equally simple: Let's Ride. I chose a light green for the background to touch on the environmental benefits of cycling and also because, as we all know, green means go. Cutting carbon can be fun, too—get a crew and let's ride!" –JH

Designed for PowertothePoster.org, 2009; modified for Green Patriot Posters, 2010.

GO FURTHER: criticalmass.wikia.com/wiki/List_of_rides

LETS DO THIS

JEREMY DEAN | Let's Do This

"Jeremy Dean's poster is a contemporary take on the classic Rosie the Riveter poster We Can Do It!_, which was one of the primary inspirations for the Green Patriot Poster project."_ –DS and EM

GO FURTHER: theyesmen.org

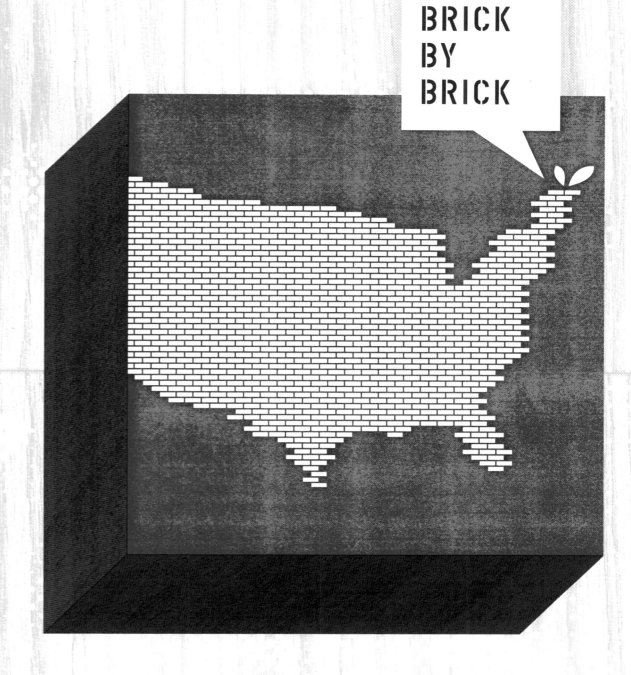

CALLOUSED HAND BY CALLOUSED HAND   greenpatriotposters.org

JUSTIN KEMERLING | (Re)Make America

"I think about the idea of America a lot. The history of things. How we got here and where we want to go. It's been a long process in working toward becoming the land of opportunity with freedom and justice for all, and the whole bit. And we have such a long way to go.

"It's brick by brick. It's DIY. So pick up your talents and get to it. Until your hands hurt. This image of 'America in bricks' found its way into my design work, really speaking to the idea that many parts make a whole. Optimistic. Hopeful. Good reason to get your hands calloused.

"The design was originally part of the Power to the Poster project. The purpose of Power to the Poster is to bring people together around a ready supply of well-designed, wild postings that comment on the issues of our time. The posters are for anyone, anywhere, to download, print, and post, centered around the question, 'As a global citizen, what moves you?'

"Now, you can call sustainability a movement. That's a clear sign things are getting better. And it's quickly approaching 'the way things must be because that's the way it is' with complete infiltration into every aspect of everything—energy, food, buildings, transportation, and on and on. It's as if we're approaching this grand realization. Deep down we know we can't carry on like this. With such levels of pollution, inequality, and injustice, we'll all collectively have the 'aha' moment, get a grip, and use our vast quantities of creativity to remake America and our world community into a bright place for everyone to call home.

"It's definitely a good time to be out there making noise." –JK

Designed for PowertothePoster.org, 2009; modified for Green Patriot Posters, 2010.

GO FURTHER: www.bluegreenalliance.org, www.powertotheposter.org

SAVE ENERGY

Unplug

AND SPEND TIME WITH YOUR FAMILY!

CHESTER JENKINS AND TRACY JENKINS, VILLAGE | Unplug

"We're a family of three living in an apartment in a city, which makes our carbon footprint pretty small to start with. We don't drive or fly much, we work from home, and most of our errands are run on foot in our neighborhood and the neighborhood next to ours. One way we can increase our greenness is by turning the computers and televisions off, and just spending time together as a family." –CJ and TJ

GO FURTHER: www.nrdc.org/air/energy/genergy/easy.asp

SIMPLICITY
IS THE KEY TO
SUCCESSFUL LIVING

NICK DEWAR (1973–2010) | Simplicity Is the Key to Successful Living

"I hope that America is entering a post–'greed is good' period. I can't think of a single step that would change the nature of our society more than everyone abandoning their automobiles and cycling instead. There would be less dependence on oil, obesity levels would drop dramatically, and reflective bike clips would replace fancy ladies' purses as the current must-have fashion accessory." –ND

Design appeared in *Readymade* magazine, 2009.

GO FURTHER: www.transalt.org

VIER5 | Umwelt

"Green ist Pantone 802." –Vier5

GO FURTHER: www.bruno-latour.fr

JMR | Rejuve a Nation

"*From the* New York Times:

"*'In a plan that would drastically remake New York City's skyline and shores, Mayor Michael R. Bloomberg is seeking to put wind turbines on the city's bridges and skyscrapers and in its waters as part of a wide-ranging push to develop renewable energy' (http://www.nytimes. com/2008/08/20/nyregion/20windmill.html).*

"*Coincidentally, Bloomberg came out with this proposal after my design. Or maybe because of it.*" –JMR

GO FURTHER: www.nyc.gov/html/planyc2030/html/home/home.shtml

CHRIS SIALS NEAL | Eat Local, Buy Local, Grow Local!

"Solving the world's energy and food problems would do a great deal to strengthen the global economy, prevent disease, and reverse the effects of climate change. The original victory garden program was designed to ease pressure on the public agricultural supply and support the war effort by encouraging families to grow their own food. I wanted to expand this idea to the broader concept of buying and eating local food." –CSN

Design appeared in *Readymade* magazine, 2009.

GO FURTHER: slowfood.com

Detroit

As

Let

the great world

SPIN

Refrain

forever

down the

ringing

grooves

of change

PAUL ELLIMAN | Detroit as Refrain

"The line of text is by Alfred, Lord Tennyson (an old friend of mine!), and the images are a sequence from a film (commissioned and subsequently suppressed by Chrysler Corp. in 1957) by the great Len Lye. For the anticapitalists among us, Detroit represents much more than just the beginning of the end for a sinister form of economic production; it represents the start of a new age in which the Detroit National Park becomes the first city under the aegis of the National Park Service (U.S. Department of the Interior), circa 2025—those being the kind of grooves of perpetual change that Tennyson recognizes in the first steam engine that thunders past him circa 1835, tho' that's not to deny him the same affection for Omar S or Carl Craig that I have!" –PE

GO FURTHER: sustainabledetroit.org

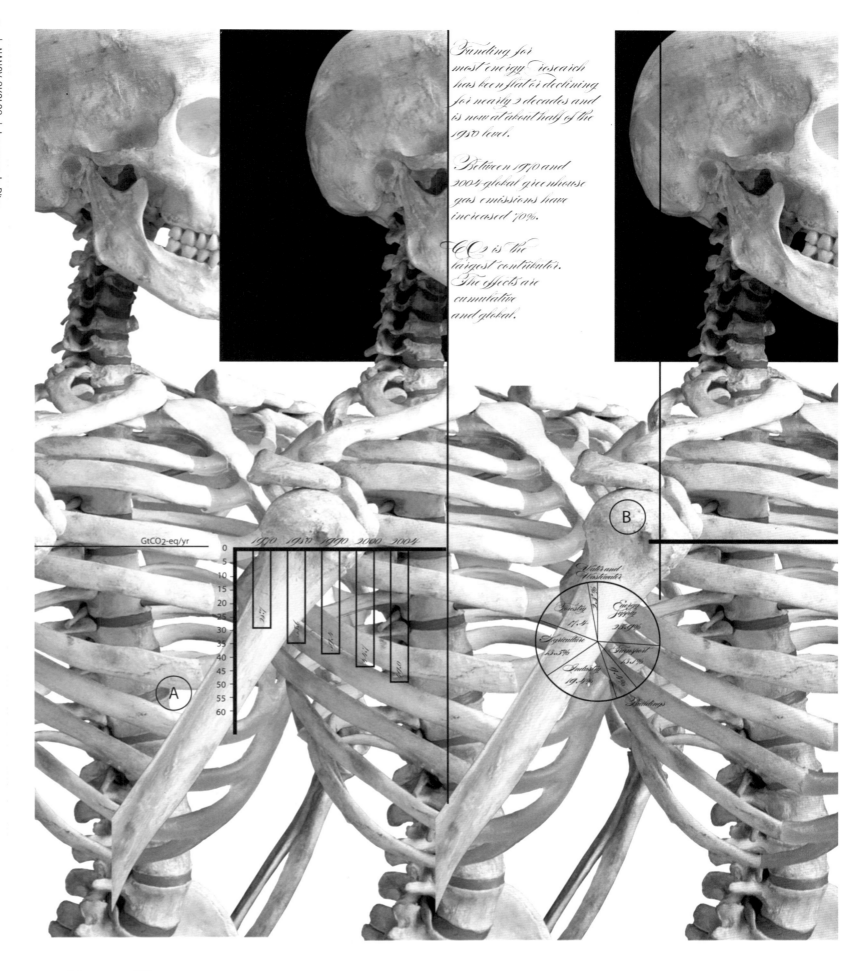

Funding for most energy research has been flat or declining for nearly 3 decades and is now at about half of the 1980 level.

Between 1970 and 2004 global greenhouse gas emissions have increased 70%.

CO_2 is the largest contributor. The effects are cumulative and global.

How ignorance is bliss, 'tis folly to be wise.

GREEN PATRIOT POSTERS

Information Source
IPCC AR4 Synthesis Report
Intergovernmental Panel
on Climate Change (IPCC) www.ipcc.ch

Quotation from Adam Gray
set in Burgues Script
Poster Design and Photography
Skolos-Wedell 2009

NANCY SKOLOS | Ignorance Is Bliss

"An Inconvenient Truth *provided initial phrases for poster concepts. These included 'wake up,' 'day of reckoning,' '+ CO_2 = + temperature,' and 'has no face.' The poster is an attempt at a gentle yet jarring image of humankind ignorantly killing itself. The text and graphs illustrate dramatically rising carbon emission levels.*" –NS

GO FURTHER: www.epa.gov/climatechange/science/index.html

problem

ME

solution

ME

You started it, you can solve it. Stop global warming today.

STEVE LE | Problem Me, Solution Me

"For a problem that was caused by us, we have the ability to clean up our mess and solve global warming. It is our world; we should treat it with the utmost care." –SL

GO FURTHER: www.green-e.org/base/re_products

MEREDITH STERN, JUSTSEEDS | We Are Power

"When I made this print I had started thinking a lot about sustainability and natural power. I was thinking of Energizer bunnies and the ridiculous notion of batteries (or any energy) that go on and on and on without considering the environmental consequences of our energy consumption. One of the very first stencils I made was of a rabbit with the heading, 'Sneaky and quick does the trick'; for me it was about toppling capitalism in subtle yet effective ways. I was looking to create a new print that incorporated some of the same ideas—of sneaky rabbits causing havoc. It also alludes a bit to the 'nature versus machine' tension that exists within our unsustainable culture.

"Technically this was a complicated print to make, involving a reduction-cut linoleum block, multiple woodblocks, and several layers of spray-paint stencil. The print is available for sale on the Justseeds website. Justseeds is currently creating a portfolio project titled Resourced. It brings together dozens of artists who are making prints about climate change and environmental issues. Each artist worked with an environmental justice organization to create an image that can be used by the organization to highlight issues it addresses in its work. The images will be distributed around the world as the organizations use them in the promotion of their work, in fund-raising campaigns, as clip art for their websites, and so on." –MS

GO FURTHER: www.justseeds.org

# "You Shouldn't Have!"

**Be kind to your parents.
Give something back.**

JON-PAUL VILLEGAS | You Shouldn't Have

"The poster uses the metaphor of kinship as a strategy for bridging the emotional disconnect that allows for the intellectual abstraction of natural systems and hence their eventual disregard in the mind of the viewer. Through the introduction of familiar emotional tropes, the viewer is invited to see his or her relationship with the natural world as a personal one based on themes of conscience, empathy, sacrifice, and commitment." –JPV

GO FURTHER: www.eowilson.org

buy local

for your health, environment, and country

JESSICA COLALUCA, SEED | Buy Local

"Buying locally reduces our carbon footprint, bolsters local industry, and focuses our attention on making healthy and ethical food choices. The Buy Local poster's design was inspired by the fact that Detroit Metro Airport had recently bought the last remaining parcel of what had been my family's farm, thus ending our farming history. The farm, which the airport purchased gradually over several decades, was a place the extended family sent their children to be fed during the Great Depression and where my grandmother raised her children while my grandfather was off fighting in World War II. For me the ominous factors of air transit physically ending local farming through land acquisition and the airline industry's environmental impact are offset by optimism inspired by my grandmother's legacy and era. The effect is a call to reclaim our values, history, and responsibility." –JC

GO FURTHER: www.foodincmovie.com

EFFORTS *Up!*

CARBON *Down!*

GREEN
PATRIOT
POSTERS

RYAN ARRUDA | Efforts Up! Carbon Down!

"I was very struck by the notion that climate change has the power to affect not only our environmental conditions but our social parameters as well; indeed, democracy itself is threatened by the chaos that unchecked climate change promises to bring. As democracy is a hallmark of our American identity, I felt that drawing attention to its precarious situation in the face of climate change would resonate with a mass audience.

"My goal was to create a classic-looking and bold graphic statement. I wanted the visual elements to be secondary to the typographic imperative. Succinct slogans—such as 'This Cannot Wait,' 'Sustainable Resources Sustain Democracy,' and 'Efforts Up! Carbon Down!'—coupled with simple renderings of national symbols (such as the United States Capitol) helped reinforce the authority and urgency of the message." –RA

Designed for Green Patriot Posters studio in bachelor of graphic design program at Rhode Island School of Design, 2009, taught by Nancy Skolos and critiqued by Edward Morris.

GO FURTHER: www.climate.org/topics/climate-change/pentagon-study-climate-change.html

2000 2005 2010
2015 2020 2025
2030 2035 2040
2045 2050 2055
2060 2065 2070
2075

OUR WATER IS RISING — RISE UP TO STOP IT.

Scientists project that sea levels will rise between 2.5 to 6.5 feet by 2100.*
Act now to stop the climate crisis. Visit canary-project.org

ROB GIAMPIETRO / GREENPATRIOTPOSTERS.ORG

*Kinematic Constraints on Glacier Contributions to 21st-Century Sea-Level Rise, W. T. Pfeffer, J. T. Harper, and S. O'Neel (5 September 2008) Science 321 (5894), 1340. [DOI: 10.1126/science.1159099]

ROB GIAMPIETRO | Water's Rising

"As it was for so many, Al Gore's An Inconvenient Truth was a huge wake-up call for me. In that film Gore offered many hard facts that highlight the urgency of our current situation, but one stood out: He suggested sea levels could rise twenty feet or more 'in the near future,' placing a sizable portion of the world at risk of being underwater by the end of the century. While recent reports have adjusted Gore's estimate—a 2008 study in the journal Science projects a rise of 2.5 to 6.5 feet by 2100—even that more modest increase is significant, potentially affecting 145 million people or more.

"My poster attempts to visualize this uncertain future, counting off the century in five-year increments and showing how quickly and completely our landscape could be altered if we do not act now to stop it. Formally I was thinking back to Emil Ruder's experiments with harmonic shifts in type size in the 1960s. The poster uses Compacta, a typeface designed by Fred Lambert that dates from the same time period as Ruder's work and which I've used in many of my own recent personal projects. The Bulletin of the Atomic Scientists' Doomsday Clock, aka 'Six Minutes to Midnight,' was very much in my mind as well. I've always thought that graphic is a stark, stirring reminder of the price of apathy." –RG

GO FURTHER: www.sciencemag.org/cgi/content/abstract/321/5894/1340

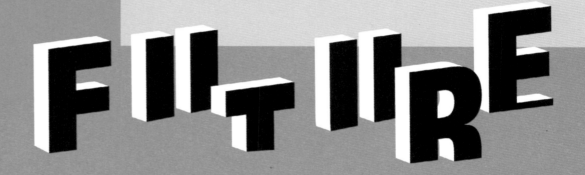

LAUREN PERLOW | S.O.S.

"We looked for posters that communicated even at thumbnail size. This design from Lauren Perlow fit the bill. It's immediately graspable. The idea of witnessing a drowning is horrible. Who wouldn't try to help—even when the drowning thing is as abstract as the 'Future'?" –DS and EM

GO FURTHER: en.wikipedia.org/wiki/Stern_Review

Take shorter showers

$99 per year just by taking fewer minutes to wash.

Save 350 lbs. of carbon dioxide per year and...

Showers account for 2/3 of all water heating costs.

ERIN PUGLIESE | Shorter Showers

"With everyone discussing sustainability, global warming, and how important it is to save the environment, it is essential that people be informed about the beneficial changes they can make. I chose to design a poster focusing on water conservation. It's amazing how so simple an act as shortening the length of your shower can make such a major impact when we all participate. There are many different ways to help conserve the Earth's resources, and most of them will save you money in the process! With nothing to lose and so much to gain, why not join in the effort?" –EP

GO FURTHER: sustainablechoices.stanford.edu/actions/in_the_home/shortshowers.html

WATER

POWER
IS READY

ARE YOU?

TELL YOUR CONGRESSMAN, UTILITY COMPANY AND HARDWARE STORE
WHEN YOU ARE READY TO MAKE THE SWITCH TO RENEWABLE ENERGY
EXPLORE YOUR OPTIONS BY VISITING GREENPATRIOTPOSTERS.ORG

SINCLAIR SMITH | Water Power Is Ready

"This poster is from a triptych that presents sun, water, and wind as immediately available sources of renewable energy and emphasizes consumer responsibility for their adoption and success in curbing global warming. The images are inspired by the power and simplicity of the first of three series of iconic posters that Lester Beall made in 1937 for the Rural Electrification Administration, and by World War II–era propaganda aimed at citizen action." –SS

GO FURTHER: library.thinkquest.org/26663/en/4_2_2.html

CO_2

One-third of
all animal species
are at risk of
extinction by 2050
unless greenhouse
gas emissions
are reduced by 30%

JOE SCORSONE AND ALICE DRUEDING | Consequences of CO_2

"We are all tied to the well-being of a planet that is threatened by CO_2 emissions poisoning the atmo-sphere. The fate of animals, a third of which will be extinct by 2050, foretells the fate of humans unless there is a worldwide commitment to reducing greenhouse gases.

"This poster was designed to create awareness of the problem of CO_2 emissions. It was selected by the 2009 GOOD 50x70 poster competition, exhibited in Milan, Italy, and will be made available to environmental organizations around the world." –JS and AD

Designed for the GOOD 50x70 poster competition, 2009.

GO FURTHER: www.nature.com/nature/journal/v427/n6970/abs/nature02121.html

VICTORY NOW

PLANT A GARDEN TODAY

GREEN PATRIOT POSTERS

SOW

CULTIVATE

THRIVE

BEN BARNES | Sow

"Sow Cultivate Thrive is a poster series developed around the concept of the victory garden posters of World War II, with a modern interpretation. Stylistically I wanted them to have an American militaristic feel with the idea of taking action to plant a garden." –BB

GO FURTHER: www.fritzhaeg.com/garden/initiatives/edibleestates/main.html

PLENTY OF
——————
IN THE SEA

BAGS OF JOY | Plenty Of

"*This poster was designed to create awareness of mass industrial fishing. A new global study con-cludes that 90 percent of all large fishes have disappeared from the world's oceans in the past half century, the devastating result of industrial fishing. In the future, fish could be a thing of the past.*"
–Bags of Joy

GO FURTHER: wwf.panda.org/about_our_earth/aboutcc/search_climate_news_resources/?50460

ADAM GRAY | Join the Revolution

"Both the bike and the heart icon seem to have currency at the moment. Gray combined both in this design, which evokes a peaceful sort of revolutionary vigor." –DS and EM

GO FURTHER: www.copenhagencyclechic.com

MARLENA BUCZEK SMITH | Oil Spill Gulf of Mexico 2010

"The voice of the image extends in diverse ways, becoming the open sound of awareness for a greater cause than one's personal fulfillment." –MBS

GO FURTHER: www.endoil.org

XANDER POLLOCK | Shit Be Meltin'

"Al Gore is right: Shit be meltin'. Would his melting face be more convincing than factual charts and graphs? How much proof do we need before we make a change?" –DS and EM

GO FURTHER: www.realclimate.org/index.php/archives/2005/03/worldwide-glacier-retreat

IF YOU'RE COMPLAINING ABOUT MY TONE THEN YOU DON'T UNDERSTAND THE MAGNITUDE OF THE PROBLEM

ANDREW SLOAT | If You Don't Like My Tone

"Eat less meat. Fly less. Take your garbage seriously. Understand the mechanics of policy-making and vote in all elections. Participate in local government. Take the bus. Have fewer children. And so on. Don't be afraid to be a pain about this stuff." –AS

GO FURTHER: www.adbusters.org/magazine/89

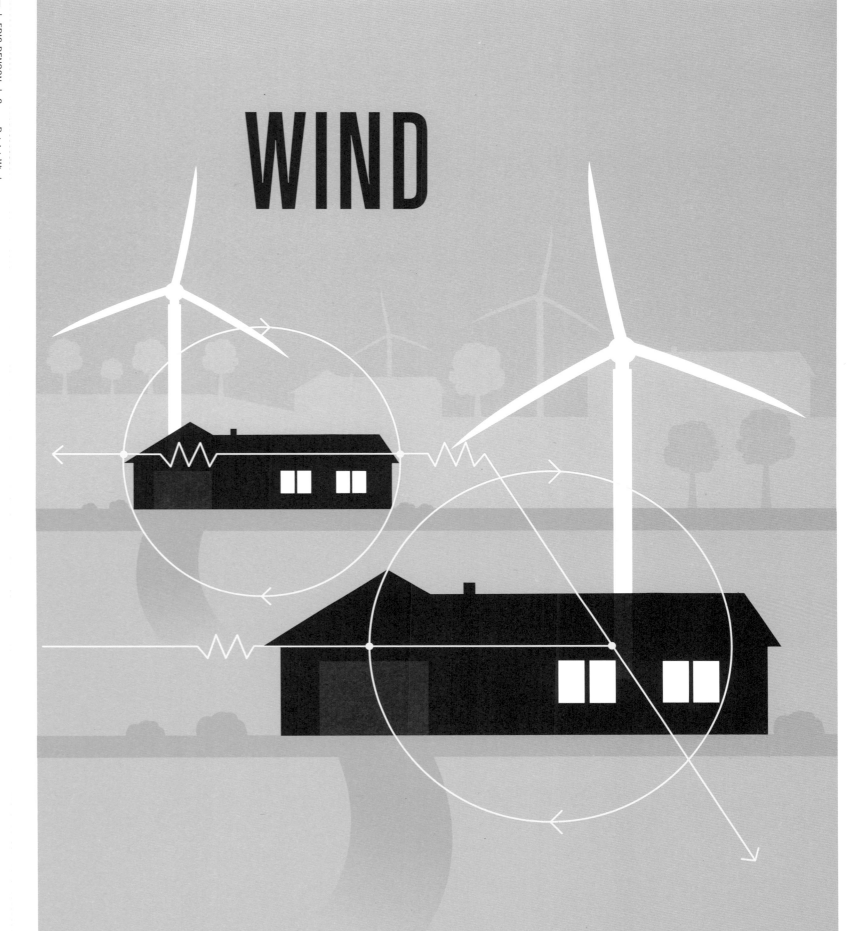

WIND

RENEWABLE ELECTRIFICATION ADMINISTRATION

ERIC BENSON | Green Patriot Wind

"*With the election of a new American president in 2008 pushing for a greener economy and a revitalization of our country's infrastructure, I was reminded of the WPA posters made between 1936 and 1943 as part of FDR's New Deal. My hopeful Renewable Electrification Administration posters are a twenty-first-century upgrade paying homage to Lester Beall's Rural Electrification Administration posters from 1937.*" –EB

GO FURTHER: www.whitehouse.gov/issues/energy-and-environment

c. 2050

KEO PIERRON | c. 2050

"Unless we keep global warming under 2 degrees Celsius [3.6 Fahrenheit] by 2050, as many as one-third of all animal species may be at risk of extinction, and as many as four billion people may be without vital sources of water. Humankind must make a heartfelt commitment to reducing carbon dioxide emissions in order to prevent our demise. Otherwise there will only be one outcome for humanity, as well as for every innocent animal species on Earth." –KP

GO FURTHER: www.oxfam.org/en/pressroom/pressrelease/2010-01-29/four-billion-threatened-water-shortages-climate-change-hurdle

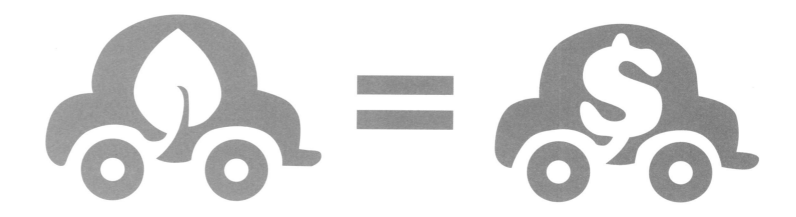

SARA STRYJEWSKI | Being Green

"Hybrid cars are getting cheaper, and being less reliant on fossil fuels is imperative. If more people bought green cars, we could be rollin' in it." –SS

GO FURTHER: www.hybridcars.com

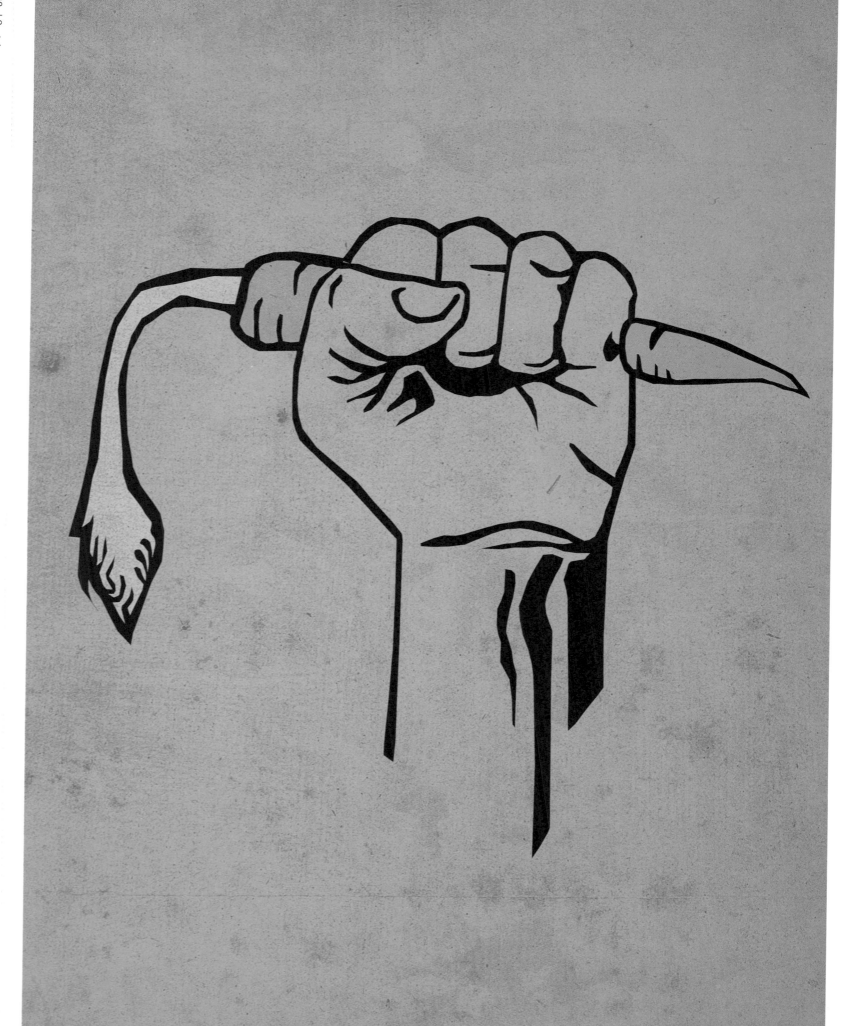

WILL ETLING | Sustain

"Young farmers need to be politically organized and active. Growing up in rural California, I always had a tremendous respect for the few remaining working farmers in our community. When my dad was in high school, he would load and haul hay bales in the summers. When I was a kid he'd play me Ry Cooder's song 'The Taxes on the Farmer Feeds Us All' and describe the backbreaking labor of hauling hay. In this poster I tried to convey the power of farming and the respect I feel for it." –WE

Design first appeared in *GOOD* magazine, 2010.

GO FURTHER: www.misa.umn.edu/vd/bfarmers.html

STEP ON IT

FELIX SOCKWELL | Step on It

"I like simple, clear messaging. Because, like too many Americans, I'm kinda dumb. But that doesn't make me any less of a patriot. I ride my homemade rickshaw to the supermarket (Trader Joe's) and to soccer games. I joined our local CSA (Rogowski Farms) and I planted a garden and taught my kids how to tend it. I compost everything. When you live conservatively and eat naturally, that's called being healthy. I know it sounds kinda dumb. But try it. It's never too late to step on it." –FS

GO FURTHER: www.carbonfootprint.com

paint it white.

...a simple solution to mitigate climate change

ADAM McBRIDE | Paint It White

"Lighter-colored surfaces within our urban environments will likely decrease climate temperatures if implemented on a global scale and at a minimum will decrease the so-called urban heat-island effect. I launched a campaign that featured this poster and others posted throughout Kansas City. My aim was to promote and educate people on the advantages of lighter surfaces in urban areas and how wide use of lighter surfaces and green roofs can benefit both our economy and our environment." –AM

GO FURTHER: www2.ucar.edu/news/computer-model-demonstrates-white-roofs-may-successfully-cool-cities

RYAN DUMAS | Eat Local

"I tried to take a lighter approach and focus on a specific action. Eating locally grown produce is not only good for the environment; it also helps build communities...and is quite tasty!" –RD

GO FURTHER: www.nal.usda.gov/afsic/pubs/csa/csa.shtml

GLOBAL
EXCESS

GUILLERMO BROTON | Global Excess
_____

"As graphic designers we have the opportunity to use our skills and tools to say something, to react, to criticize. Initiatives like the International Poster and Graphic Design Festival of Chaumont are great because they encourage designers from around the world to use their talent and imagination to create posters about different environmental, social, and cultural issues. It is also a reminder that design is not all about advertising, marketing, and brand development but can also be about more useful, lasting, and democratic communication._

"Global Excess is my response to the global warming issue. It was selected at the 2007 Chaumont festival." –GB

Designed for the International Poster and Graphic Design Festival of Chaumont, 2007.
_____

GO FURTHER: www.rmi.org/rmi

GREEN PATRIOT POSTERS.ORG

PHILLIP CLARK | Dirty Secret

"Oil is over. When will we learn?" –PC

GO FURTHER: www.earthpolicy.org

JAMES VICTORE | Save the Plants

"Why isn't this shit important?

"When I was a kid in the sixties, the tag line 'Save the planet' belonged to Superman comics. Now, forty years later, it is a reality. We have had forty years to plan and to fix and implement, but all we have done is squander. In the last forty years we have even found new ways to squander. It is fatally sad that we have to use that tag line in such a serious tone today. It is completely feeble and depressing that we as designers are supposed to be on the front line of saving the world—although we completely had a hand in giving this beautiful Earth up to the grim reaper. The reason the world is fucked—and I mean fucked, the horses have left the barn, no use in choosing 'green' inks now—is that business is too far gone and someone has to pay. And it ain't gonna be business that pays. It will be my son, Luca, who is thirteen, and his brave and strong sons.

"This is important.

"Forget the few brave and smart companies that make an effort. Why not ask the design firms who design new antiperspirant campaigns and packages (NOT actually new antiperspirants) why they perennially add new and useless crap to the shelves. The sad answer is that they get paid. They add more garbage and have no opinion whatsoever. And this is even hailed as 'good' in our business. Like that cute, smart fuck who heads Coke design. We trot him on stage like a herald and savior—all he does is sell sugar water to fat people. And the crowd roars. This is our conundrum as designers. We are so afraid of biting the hand that feeds us. And the stand of one individual against this deluge of crap is useless, because there is some young, cute, smart bastard ready to take the job just for the money. This is what business has left to us and future generations. And anyone who denies this is not only wearing blinders but is full of shit. Or just struggling to pay the rent.

"I am embarrassed that I take this situation seriously (ergo my vehement response) and am personally hurt by what we as a culture have done to this planet.

"I could go on, but it is useless, so I, as a designer, choose my battles, and take them fucking seriously.

"I hope your book makes a dent. I am in." –JV

Design originally made for Aveda, 2006.

GO FURTHER: www.timeforclimatejustice.org

NOEL DOUGLAS | Dead End

"I work within the tradition of engaged graphic communication that feeds larger social and political movements. In particular I am involved in what has been called the 'Movement of Movements,'— the anticapitalist movement, which flowered after the riots against the WTO conference in Seattle in 1999.

"The developing climate justice movement is rooted in that core anticapitalist belief. We lay the blame of climate change broadly, and the failure of the COP15 talks in Copenhagen more specifi- cally, on industrial capitalism. Going forward we look to influence the COP16 meeting in Mexico by any means necessary, and to build a global people's movement to stop climate change in the process.

"Dead End is part of a body of work made for the street protests that occupied the road outside the Carbon Trading Banks during the G20 Summit in London in 2009. These posters were also used on the streets in Copenhagen during COP15 and in Bolivia during the People's Summit. We also gave away graphic stickers during these protests.

"Images, icons, and graphic forms of communication can foreground the deathly contradictions of capitalism or open windows onto new worlds, but they must serve human and not commercial needs." –ND

GO FURTHER: www.weareeverywhere.org

(TOP) STEFAN SAGMEISTER, MATTHIAS ERNSTBERGER, RICHARD THE / SAGMEISTER, INC. (BOTTOM) MICHAEL BIERUT / PENTAGRAM WITH THE CANARY PROJECT (OVERLEAF) BANKSY

I DON'T
GLOBAL

Project director: Diana Murphy
Design and production: Dmitri Siegel
Editorial assistant: Ryan Arruda
Design assistant: Diego Gutiérrez
Separations and printing: Monroe Litho, Rochester, New York

Set in Franklin Gothic and Bureau Grotesque
Text printed on Mohawk Via PC100 Cool White (100% PCW Recycled);
cover printed on Mohawk Loop Antique Vellum 80%
PC White (80% PCW Recycled)

Thomas L. Friedman's "The Power of Green" first appeared in the
New York Times Magazine on April 15, 2007, and is excerpted by
permission of Thomas L. Friedman.

First published in the United Kingdom in 2011 by
Thames & Hudson Ltd, 181A High Holborn,
London WC1V 7QX

British Library Cataloguing-in-Publication Data
A catalogue record for this book is available from the British Library

ISBN: 978-0-500-28926-6

First published in the United States of America in 2010 by
Metropolis Books

D.A.P./Distributed Art Publishers
155 Sixth Avenue, 2nd floor
New York, NY 10013
tel 212 627 1999
fax 212 627 9484
www.artbook.com
and
Metropolis Magazine
61 West 23rd Street, 4th floor
New York, NY 10010
tel 212 627 9977
fax 212 627 9988
www.metropolismag.com

A portion of the proceeds from the sale of this book
will support the work of The Canary Project.

To find out about all our publications, please visit
www.thamesandhudson.com.
There you can subscribe to our e-newsletter, browse or download our current
catalogue, and buy any titles that are in print.

Acknowledgments

*It would not have been possible to print this book using sustainable
practices (see "Destroy This Book") without generous contributions
from the Environmental Defense Fund, Richard H. Goodwin, Judith
Bell, Neva Goodwin, Gabe Nugent, Hiscock & Barclay, and an
anonymous source.*

*We would also like to thank Diana Murphy for her vision and
determination in seeing this book through; David Steinman of
Green Patriot and Freedom Press for the use of the name "Green
Patriot"; Michael Bierut for launching the project with his extremely
successful campaign of bus advertisements; John Caserta for
designing the Green Patriot website; Shepard Fairey and Studio
Number One for their great generosity and genuine commitment
to the cause; Aaron Perry Zucker and Adam Meyer for designing
the Make a Poster section of the website, and Aaron for helping
produce the initial book proposal; Diego Gutiérrez for last-minute
and always good-spirited help with the layout; Nancy Skolos for
her tremendous faith in the project, the results of which were
a dedicated studio in the bachelor of graphic design program
at the Rhode Island School of Design and several of the posters
presented here; Ryan Arruda, a student in that studio who went
on to become the invaluable editorial assistant for this book;
Michelle Ha for facilitating the RISD studio; Citizen Schools for
partnering on an inspiring educational program in Boston; and,
last but certainly not least, all the designers who have submitted
ideas and images to the movement. We are just beginning.*
—DS and EM

Illustration Credits

Front cover image: Shepard Fairey / ObeyGiant.com © 2009;
front flap: Art © Estate of Robert Rauschenberg and Gemini G.E.L./
Licensed by VAGA, New York, NY. Published by Gemini G.E.L.;
p. 2: (left) Jason Hardy, *Bike Your City*, (right) Nicholas Hans and
Clint Woodside, *Mugs Are Great*; p. 4: (left) Annemarie Byrd,
Get Growing, (right) Petter Ringbom / Flat, *People Make Parks*;
pp. 6–7: courtesy Northwestern University Libraries and the
University of North Texas; pp. 20–21: (clockwise from top left)
Bernardo Margulis, Jared Hardy, Nicholas Hans and Clint Woodside,
Iain Burke, Gloria Chung, Vanessa Brown, Kelly Holohan, Sinclair
Smith, Adam Gray, Annemarie Byrd, Winterhouse, Jeremy Dean,
Bizhan Khodabandeh, Paula Chang, Jason Dietrick, Petter
Ringbom / Flat, Serafim Zahariev, Michael Doyle; p. 41: Shepard
Fairey / ObeyGiant. com © 2009; p. 123: Joseph Huff-Hannon; p.
124: HunterGatherer, Noel Douglas, Susannah Sayler / The Canary
Project, Shadia Fayne Wood; p. 125: (top) Sagmeister, Inc., (bottom)
Billy Delfs; pp. 126–27: Maggie Jones

BELIEVE IN

WARMING